Progressive
Violin
Method for Young Beginners
Book 1

by Peter Gelling

PROGRESSIVE VIOLIN METHOD FOR YOUNG BEGINNERS BOOK 1
I.S.B.N. 978 1 86469 144 3
Order Code: CP-69144

For more information on this series contact;
Koala Music Publications
email: info@learntoplaymusic.com
or visit our website;
www.learntoplaymusic.com

COPYRIGHT CONDITIONS
No part of this product can be reproduced in any form
without the written consent of the publishers.
© 2012 L.T.P. Publishing Pty Ltd

RC-EREP

Like us on Facebook
www.facebook.com/LearnToPlayMusic

View our YouTube Channel
www.youtube.com/learntoplaymusiccom

Follow us on Twitter
twitter.com/LTPMusic

Visit our Website
www.learntoplaymusic.com

Published by
KOALA MUSIC
PUBLICATIONS™

Let's Practice Together

We have recorded all the songs in this book onto a CD. When your teacher's not there, instead of practicing by yourself, you can play along with us. Practicing will be much more fun, you can hear all the correct pitches and rhythms, and you will learn faster. Each song is played twice.

- The first time contains the song with the accompaniment and your part (the melody).
- The second time contains just the accompaniment. You can play your part along with the accompaniment.
- A drum introduction is used to begin each exercise.
- At the beginning of the CD there are four tuning notes – G, D, A and E, which correspond to the open strings of the violin. It is a good idea to tune the violin to these notes before every practice session. Tuning is difficult at first, so it is best to have your teacher tune your violin whenever possible. In time, you will be able to do it yourself.

 1. Tuning Notes - G, D, A, E.

Contents

Introduction   **Page 4**

Lesson 1 Parts of the Violin   5
How to Hold the Violin   6
How to Hold the Bow   6
Pizzicato Playing   7
Playing With the Bow   8

Lesson 2 How to Read Music   9
The Staff   9
The Treble Clef   9
The Quarter Note   9
The Note A   10
Ant Walk   10
Bar Lines   10
The 4/4 Time Signature   11
Four Four Ants   11
The Note B   12
Bees and Ants   12
The Half Note   13
Half a Bee   13
The Repeat Sign   13
Halves and Quarters   13

Lesson 3 The Note C Sharp (C#)   14
Sharp Cat   14
The Half Rest   15
Chord Symbols   15
Merrily   **15**
Hot Cross Buns   **16**
The Whole Note   16
In the Light of the Moon   **16**

Lesson 4 The Note D   17
Hot Dog   17
Stepping and Skipping   18
Playing With the CD   18

Lesson 5 The Note E   19
Elephant Talk   19
The C time signatures   20

My House   **20**
Lightly Row   **21**

Lesson 6 The 3/4 Time Signature   22
Waltz and All   22
The Dotted Half Note   23
Dotted Waltz   23
Girls and Boys Come Out to Play   **24**
The Quarter Rest   25
Little Bo Peep   **25**

Lesson 7 The Lead-in   26
When the Saints go Marchin' In   **26**

Notes and Rests Summary   **28**

Introduction

Progressive Violin Method For Young Beginners in two books has been designed to introduce the younger student to the basics of playing the violin and reading music. To maximise the student's enjoyment and interest, the book incorporates a repertoire of well known children's songs. All of the songs have been carefully graded into an easy to follow, lesson by lesson format which assumes no prior knowledge of music by the student. Since violin is often accompanied by guitar, piano or keyboard, this book may be used in conjunction with other Progressive Young Beginner books for these instruments, as many of the songs included here are common to these other books.

At the beginning of the book, the student is introduced to the basic principles of holding the violin and bow and pizzicato and bowing techniques before tackling playing and music reading. Along the way the student learns note and rest values and the   and   time signatures. The exercises and songs incorporate quarter, whole and half notes and their equivalent rests. The student is taught how to read rhythms, and introduced to basic terms such as bar lines, repeat signs and lead-in notes. New pieces of information are highlighted by color boxes, and color illustrations are used throughout to stimulate and maintain the student's interest.

A Word About Intonation and Timing

Many young students have difficulty in playing pitches accurately. This will improve with practice and experience. It is important to understand the concept of exact pitches, but not to worry if the student has intonation problems at first. Careful listening, and playing along with the CD will help with intonation, but it is best to work on this aspect of playing with a teacher right from the beginning.

One of the most important things about learning music is developing a good sense of time. To get you on the right track from the very beginning, it is strongly recommended that you use a metronome to play along with every time you practice. There are various types of metronome available, from the old wind-up style metronome to the electronic metronome. Electronic metronomes are recommended because they are more accurate and often have a volume control as well as an earphone input so nobody else hears it except the person using it.

Lesson 1
Parts of the Violin and Bow

Look at the diagrams below and learn all the names of the parts of your violin and bow. Do this for a few minutes each day until you know them all from memory. Have your teacher or a friend test you on the names of the parts.

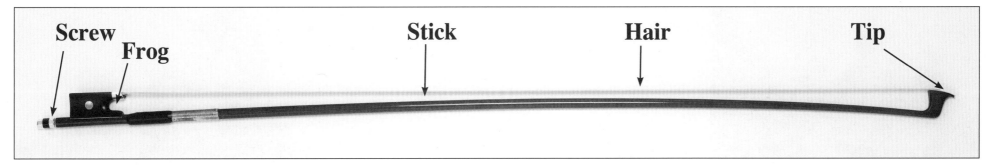

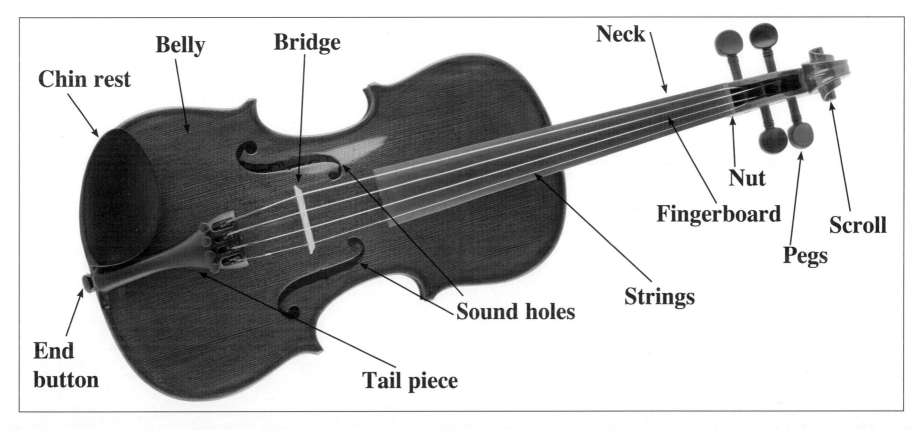

How to Hold the Violin and Bow

The correct positions for holding the violin and bow are shown in the photographs below.

Holding the Bow

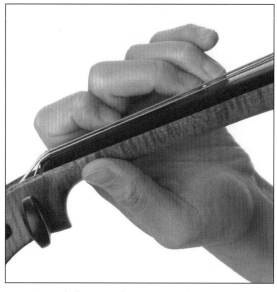

Position of the Left Hand

Holding the Violin

How to Read the Fingering Diagrams

The numbers on the fingers correspond to the numbers and letters on the note diagrams throughout the book.

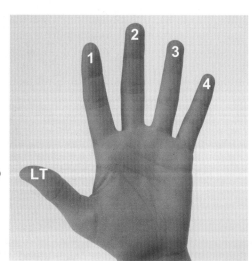

Left thumb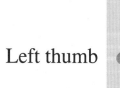

Pizzicato

A good way to begin playing the violin is to hold it in the playing position and to play the open strings **pizzicato**, which means plucking the strings with the index finger of the bowing hand. Before you begin, memorize the names of the open strings, as shown in the diagram below to the left. To play a note pizzicato, place the tip of your right thumb against the upper right corner of the fingerboard near the E string as shown in the diagram below to the right. Pluck the strings with your index finger about 5 centimeters along the fingerboard. Try plucking each of the four strings and saying the name of each string out loud as you pluck it.

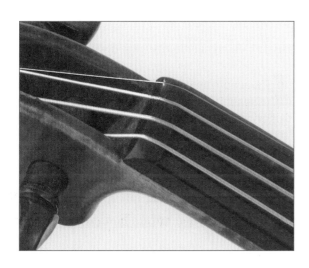  

 ## 2. Pizzicato

Practice playing the open strings pizzicato in the order shown below. The first time you play the exercise, say the names of the open strings out loud as you pluck each one. The second time you play the exercise, count **1, 2, 1, 2,** etc, and keep the notes even.

String	E	E	A	A	D	D	G	G	D	D	A	A	E	A	D	G
Count	1	2	1	2	1	2	1	2	1	2	1	2	1	2	1	2

Playing With the Bow (Arco)

Playing with the bow is called **arco** playing. This is the most common method of playing the violin. As with pizzicato, the best way to begin playing with the bow is to play just the open strings of the violin. Hold the bow in the manner described on page 6 and place the hair of the bow on the open A (2nd) string near the frog of the bow. The bow should be at right angles to the string. Draw the bow slowly across the string all the way to the tip. This is called a **down stroke**, and is indicated with the symbol ⊓. As you play you down stroke, make sure your right wrist and forearm are relaxed, as this will create the best sound. After you reach the tip of the bow, hold it steady for a moment and then slowly push the bow back across the string until you reach the frog. This is called an up stroke, which is indicated with the symbol V. Once you can produce a good sound on the open A string, try playing each of the open strings with a down stroke and then an up stroke. If you are having trouble achieving a consistent sound, you may need to rub some more rosin on the hair of the bow.

To make sure you only sound one string at a time, you will need to lower your bowing arm slightly when moving from a lower string to a higher string (e.g. open G to open D) and raise the arm slightly when moving from a higher string to a lower string (e.g. open E to open A). When moving between strings, do not lift your bow off the strings, but change the sound to the new string by changing the angle of the bow. **It is important to work on bowing technique with a teacher right from the beginning so that you do not develop any bad habits which you later have to correct.**

 ## 3. Arco

Practice playing the open strings arco in the order shown below. Count **1, 2, 1, 2,** etc, as you play, and alternate your bow strokes. Each **1 count** will be a **down stroke** with the bow and each **2 count** will be an **up stroke**.

Bow	⊓	V	⊓	V	⊓	V	⊓	V	⊓	V	⊓	V	⊓	V	⊓	V
String	E	E	A	A	D	D	G	G	D	D	A	A	E	A	D	G
Count	1	2	1	2	1	2	1	2	1	2	1	2	1	2	1	2

Lesson 2
How to Read Music

Music Notes

There are only seven letters used for notes in music. They are:

These Notes are known as the **musical alphabet**.

The Staff

These five lines are called the **staff** or **stave**.

The Treble Clef

This symbol is called a **treble clef**

There is a treble clef at the beginning of every line of most vocal music.

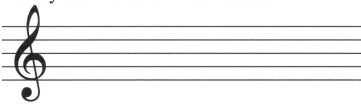

The Quarter Note

This is a musical note called a **quarter note**. It lasts for **one** beat or count.

Count: 1

Music notes are written in the spaces and on the lines of the staff

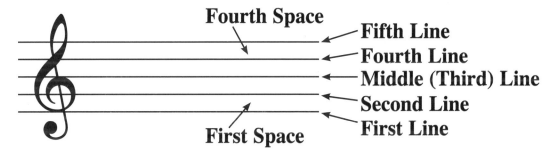

Fourth Space

Fifth Line

Fourth Line

Middle (Third) Line

Second Line

First Line

First Space

The Note A

The Note **A** is written in the second space of the staff.

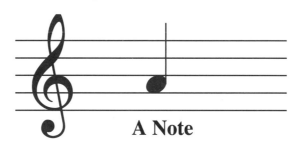

A Note

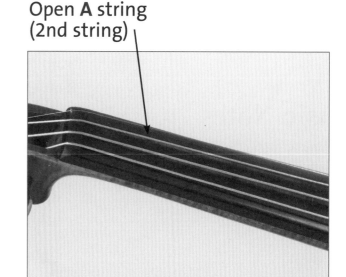

Open **A** string
(2nd string)

 ## 4. Ant Walk

In this song you will play eight **A** notes. Play the notes with the **middle** of the bow. The bow direction changes for each note. The notes on counts **1 and 3** are played with a **down stroke** and the notes on counts **2 and 4** are played with an **up stroke**. Listen carefully as you play, and try to keep the notes strong and even. It is a good idea to practice playing the notes pizzicato as well as with the bow.

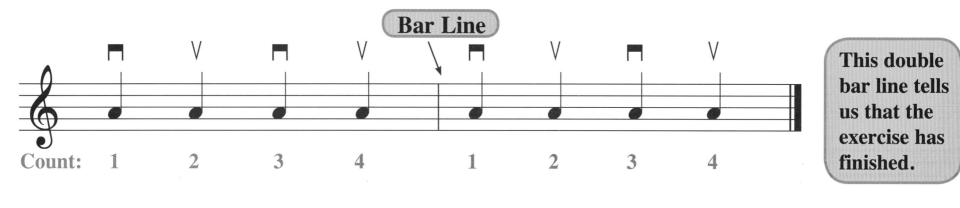

Bar Line

Count: 1 2 3 4 1 2 3 4

This double bar line tells us that the exercise has finished.

Bar Lines

Music is divided into **bars**, or **measures**, by barlines. In the first song there are two bars of music. Each bar contains four quarter notes.

The Four Four Time Signature

These two numbers are called the **four four** time signature.
They are placed after the treble clef.
The $\frac{4}{4}$ time signature tells you there are **four** beats in each
bar. There are **four** quarter notes in a bar of $\frac{4}{4}$ time.

 ## 5. Four Four Ants

This song contains four bars of quarter notes in $\frac{4}{4}$ time. On the recording there are four drumbeats to introduce songs
in $\frac{4}{4}$ time. Once again, practice this song pizzicato as well as arco (with the bow).

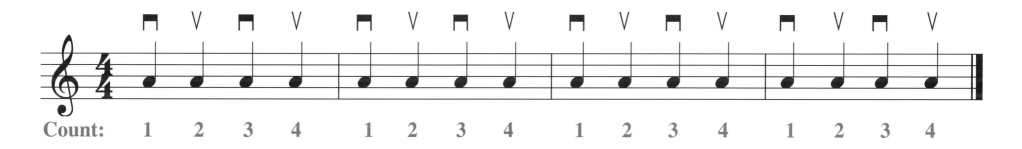

The Note B

The Note **B** is written on the third line of the staff. The stem for the note **B** can go **up or down**, because it is on the middle line of the staff.

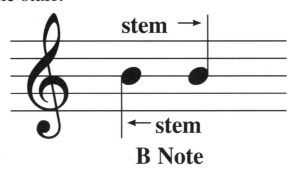

stem →

← stem

B Note

To play the note **B**, use the first finger of your left hand as shown in the diagram above. You should use the tip of your finger to hold down the string.

 ## 6. Bees and Ants

This song uses the note **B** along with the note A. Play it **pizzicato** first and then **arco**.

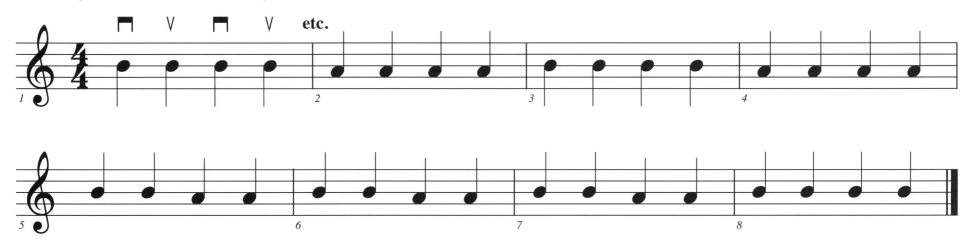

The Half Note

This is a **half** note. It lasts for **two** beats. There are two half notes in one bar of $\frac{4}{4}$ time.

Count: **1** 2

 ## 7. Half A Bee

This song contains four bars of half notes using the notes **A** and **B**. Alternate the bowing directions as shown above the notation. Half notes are played with a slower bow stroke than quarter notes.

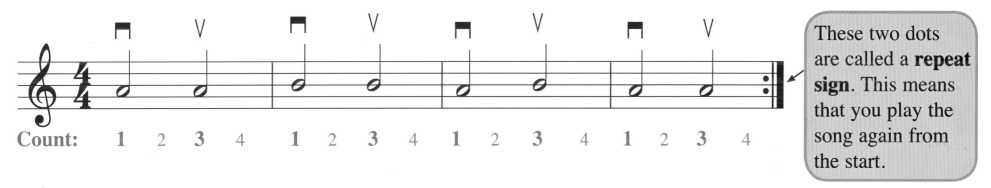

These two dots are called a **repeat sign**. This means that you play the song again from the start.

 ## 8. Halves and Quarters

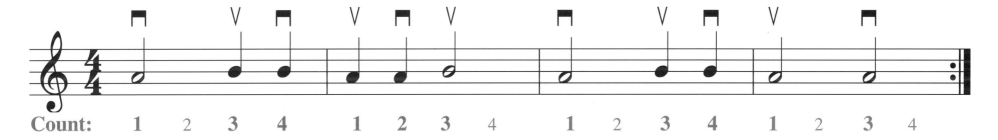

Lesson 3
The Note C Sharp (C#)

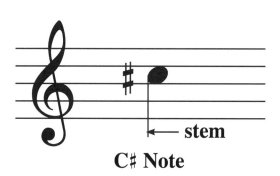

♯ This symbol is called a sharp sign.

When a sharp note is written on the staff, the sharp sign is placed **before** the note.

Notes written **above** the middle line of the staff usually have their stems going **down**.

stem ←

C♯ Note

 9. Sharp Cat

To play the note **C♯**, use the tip of the **second** finger of your left hand as shown in the diagram. As you play the **C♯**, leave your first finger in position ready to play **B** immediately afterwards. Play the song pizzicato first and then arco.

The Half Rest

Count: 1 2

A black box sitting on a line is called a **half rest**. It means there are **two beats of silence**. We place **small** counting numbers under rests.

Chord Symbols

The letters above the songs are **chord symbols**. They are not the notes you are playing. They are for your teacher or someone who is accompanying you, so they know what to play.

10. Merrily

When there is more than one sharp note in a bar, you only need to write the sharp sign before the first sharp note in that bar. A bar line cancels a sharp sign, so if there are sharps in other bars you will need a sharp sign before the first sharp note of each of those bars. This song contains a half rest in the final bar.

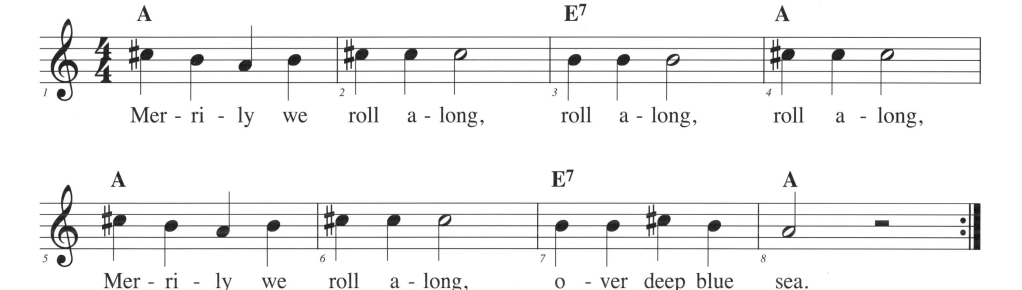

11. Hot Cross Buns

Remember to sing each new song along with the recording so you can hear how your part fits with the other instruments.

Hot cross buns, hot cross buns, hot, hot, hot cross buns.

The Whole Note

This is a **whole** note. It lasts for **four** beats. There is **one** whole note in one bar of $\frac{4}{4}$ time.

Count: 1 2 3 4

 ## 12. In the Light of the Moon

To play the whole note in the final bar of this song, you will need to use a longer, slower bow stroke.

Count: 1 2 3 4 1 2 3 4 1 2 3 4 1 2 3 4

Lesson 4
The Note D

The Note **D** is written on the **fourth** line of the staff.

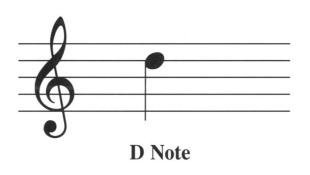

D Note

Play the note **D** with the third finger of your left hand as shown in the diagram. The space between the second and third fingers when playing **C#** and **D** is less than the space between the first and second fingers when playing **B** and **C#**. Don't worry if you have trouble with finger positions at first. With a bit of practice, your fingers will naturally go to the correct position on the fingerboard. Remember to practice your songs both pizzicato and arco.

 ### 13. Hot Dog

14. Stepping and Skipping

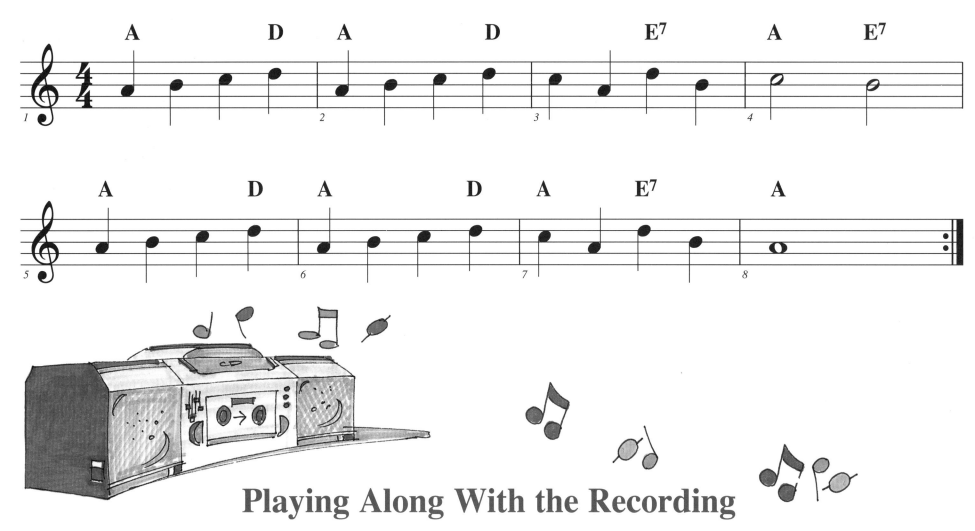

Playing Along With the Recording

Most times when you see someone playing the violin in a concert, they have other musicians playing with them. Sometimes they have just a piano or guitar, and other times it may be a whole band or an orchestra. To play well with other musicians, you need to be able to play in tune with them. A good way to practice this is to play all the songs in the book along with the recording. Listen carefully as you play with the recording to see if your notes sound the same pitch as those on the recording. If they don't, you will need to move your fingers slightly on the fingerboard either towards the nut or towards the bridge. Ask your teacher to help you with this.

Lesson 5
The Note E

The Note **E** is written 1n the fourth space of the staff.

E Note

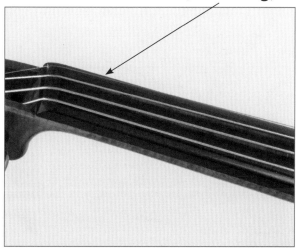

Open **E** string
(1st string)

 ## 15. Elephant Talk

The note **E** is the open first string. This song uses the note **E** along with all the notes you have learnt. Play the song pizzicato and then arco. As you move between the second and first strings, you will need to change the angle of the bow.

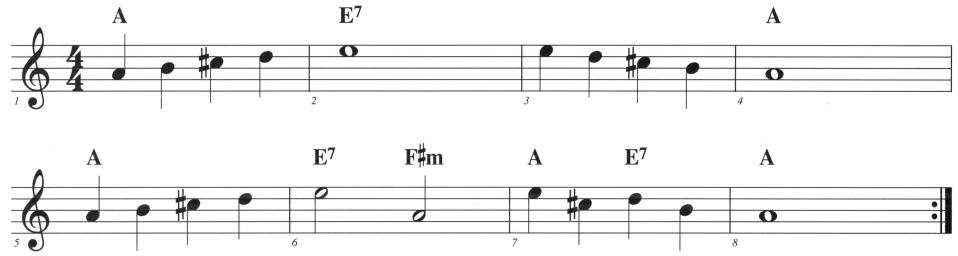

The Common Time Signature

 This symbol is called common time.
It means exactly the same as $\frac{4}{4}$.

 16. My House

Here is another song which uses the notes **A, B, C#, D** and **E**. It is a good idea to practice singing the names of the notes as you play, so you get to know them really well.

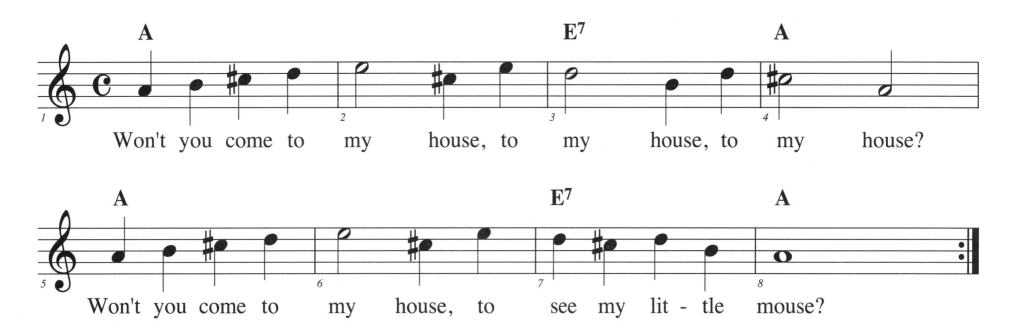

17. Lightly Row

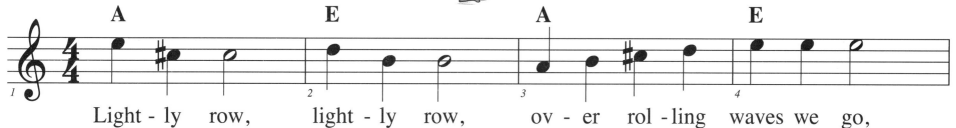

Light - ly row, light - ly row, ov - er rol - ling waves we go,

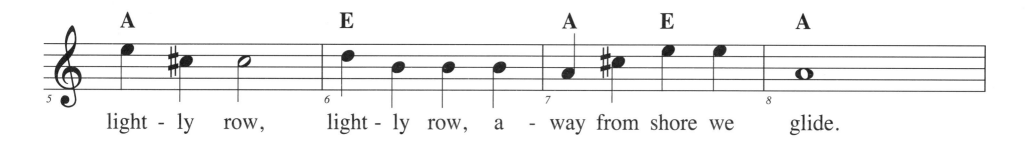

light - ly row, light - ly row, a - way from shore we glide.

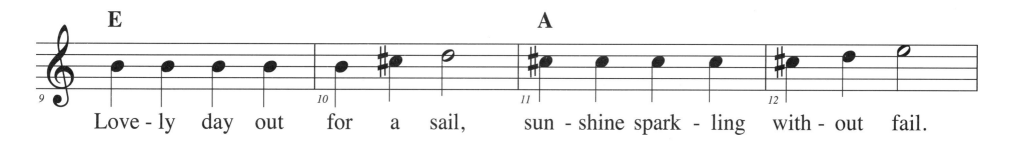

Love - ly day out for a sail, sun - shine spark - ling with - out fail.

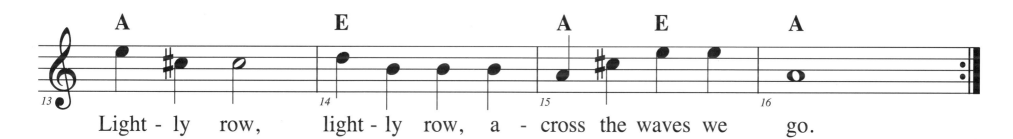

Light - ly row, light - ly row, a - cross the waves we go.

Lesson 6
The Three Four Time Signature

This is called the **three four** time signature.
It tells you there are **three** beats in each bar.
Three four time is also known as waltz time

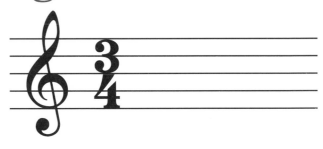

 18. Waltz and All

Before you play this song, listen to the recording and clap along with the notes, counting **1 2 3, 1 2 3** as you go. On the recording there are six drumbeats to introduce songs in $\frac{3}{4}$ time (two bars).

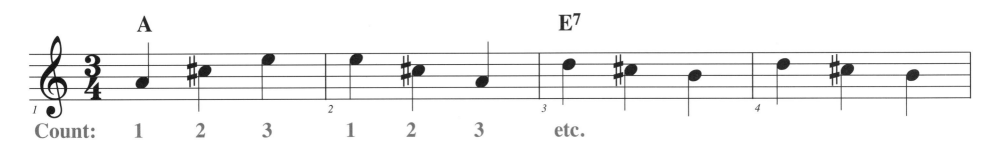

Count: 1   2   3   1   2   3   etc.

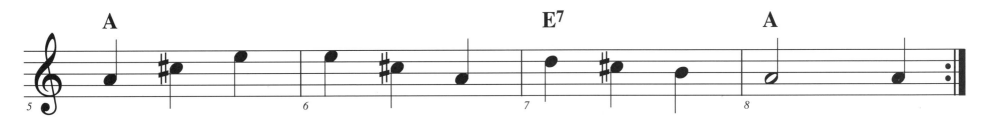

The Dotted Half Note

Count: **1** 2 3

A dot after a half note means that
you hold the note for **three** beats.

 19. Dotted Waltz

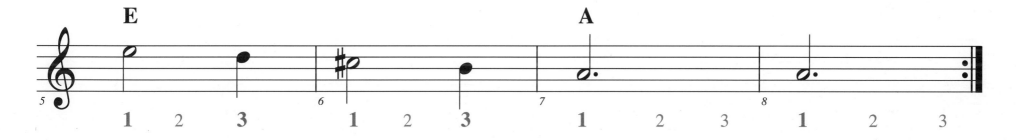

 20. Girls and Boys Come Out to Play

This song contains a dotted half note in the final bar.

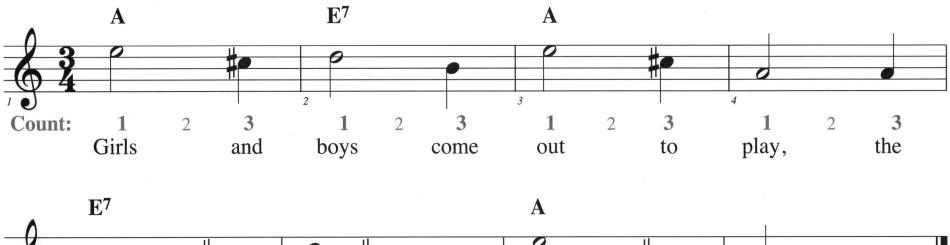

Count:
Girls and boys come out to play, the
moon is shi - ning bright as day.

The Quarter Rest

 This symbol is called a **quarter rest**.
It means there is **one beat of silence**.

Count: 1

21. Little Bo Peep

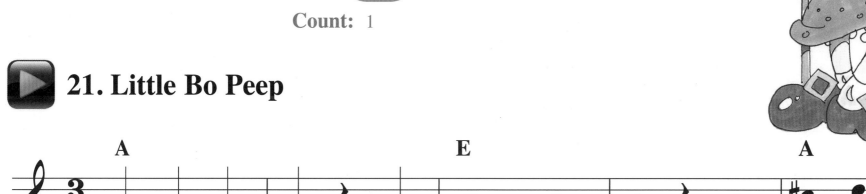

Lit - tle Bo Peep, has lost her sheep, and does'- nt know

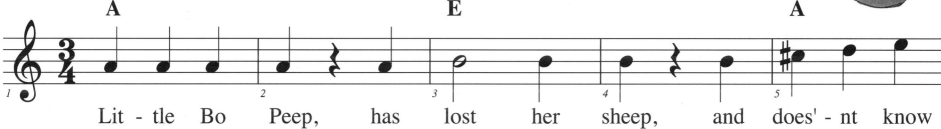

whe - re to find them, Leave them a - lone, and

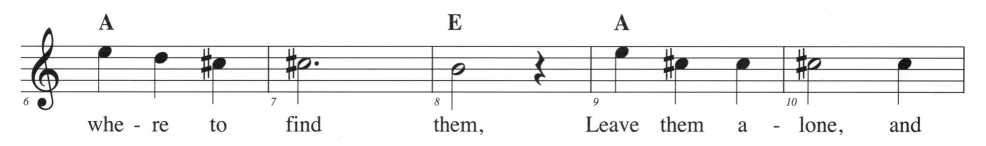

they will come home, wag - ging their tai - ls be - hind them.

Lesson 7
The Lead-in

Sometimes a song does not begin on the first beat of a bar. Any notes which come before the first full bar are called **lead-in notes** (or **pickup notes**). When we use lead-in notes, the last bar is also incomplete. The notes in the lead-in and the notes in the last bar must add up to one full bar.

22. When the Saints go Marchin' in.

There are three lead-in notes at the beginning of this song. On the recording there are **five** drumbeats to introduce this song.

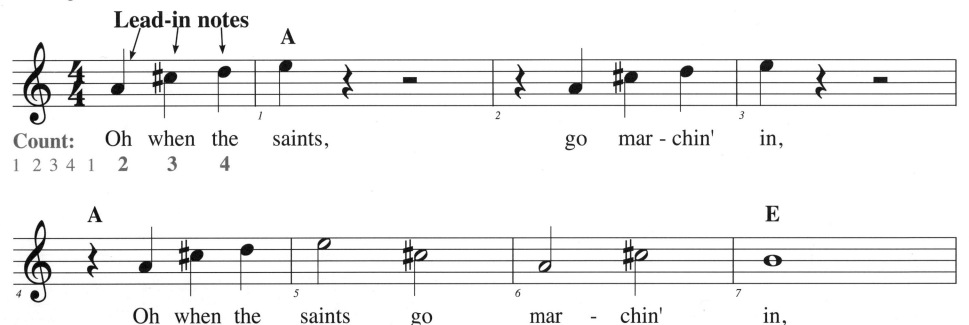

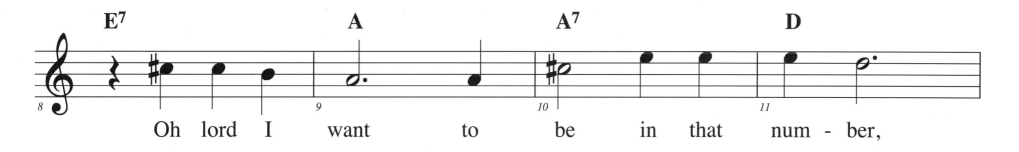

Oh lord I want to be in that num - ber,

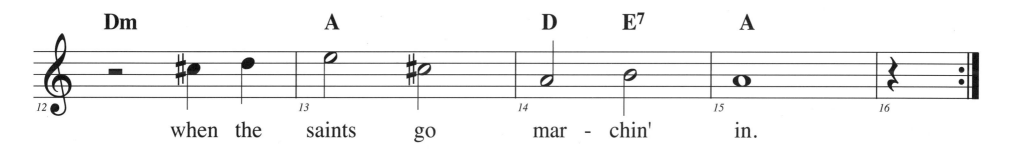

when the saints go mar - chin' in.

Notes and Rests

Name	Quarter Note (crotchet)	Half Note (minim)	Dotted Half Note (dotted minim)	Whole Note (semibreve)
Note				
Rest				
Number of Counts	1	2	3	4

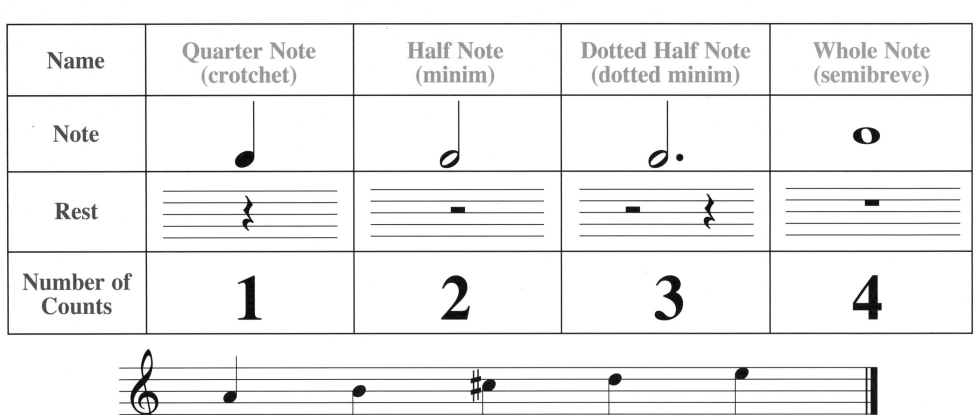

A B C# D E

Open **A** string (2nd string)

Open **E** string (1st string)

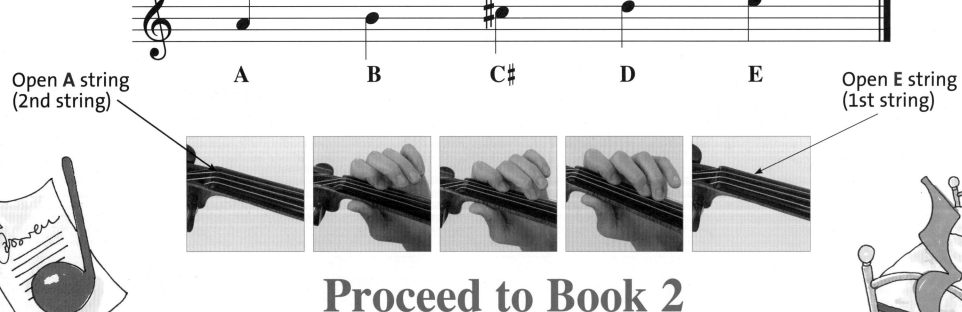

Proceed to Book 2